Truth, Integrity, Courage, Love

4 Powerful Words that Changed My Life

LaGina Glass

Balboa Press books may be ordered through booksellers or by contacting:

Balboa Press
A Division of Hay House
1663 Liberty Drive
Bloomington, IN 47403
www.balboapress.com
1-(877) 407-4847

ISBN: 978-1-4525-6452-4 (e)
ISBN: 978-1-4525-6451-7 (sc)

Printed in the United States of America

Balboa Press rev. date: 12/05/2012

YOUR ORIGINAL FACE

"Jesus said: Take no thought from the morning until the evening and from the evening until the morning, for what you shall put on.

His disciples said: When wilt thou be revealed to us and when will we see thee?

Jesus said: When you take off your clothing without being ashamed,

And take your clothes and put them under your feet as the little children

And tread on them- then shall you behold the son of the living one, and you shall not fear." (Osho 2009, 65)

CONTENTS

ACKNOWLEDGMENTS

There are a number of beautiful people who have shared my vision of the T.I.C.L. Effect and encouraged me to move forward with my life purpose to heal myself and to share my process. This journey has been guided by angels, masters, and spirit guides who speak to me intuitively and through others. To the many who have said yes when called upon by the divine to act on my behalf and to speak the very words I needed to hear in order to heal, thank you.

I extend a special thank you to my incredibly gifted soul sister Lori Waller, who has been an absolute blessing. She has connected me with life-changing teachers and resources, as well as daily coaching and encouragements. I have big love and gratitude for you. Namaste.

Thank you to my soul friend Victoria Bustillos for all those days of walking in Balboa Park and for the many moments of uncontrollable laughter. We speak our own language and I'm fortunate to be on this journey with you. We have grown in many ways and especially in our spiritual lives. You have supported me through the madness and we have celebrated many milestones together; we are forever *dos flores*.

Valerie Escalante, or as I like to refer to you, "my Val," where do we even begin? You knew me well before I knew myself …

wink, wink. We experienced career changes, financial ups and downs, and relationships. We've lived distances apart and now together again, and have never missed a beat. Thank you for joining me in bringing my dream into reality.

To my spiritual sister Cindy Montoya, from the moment we said hello, I knew you were someone who was destined to be in my life. Your genuine love and affection has melted my heart and shown me evidence of goodness in the world. We have many memories to make, and I look forward to each new day. No one loves the way you do, Boo.

INTRODUCTION

What If?

A few years ago I read Robert Schwartz's book, *Your Soul's Plan,* in which he shares stories and accounts of pre-birth planning. A pre-birth planning session is a gathering of one's soul group (a group of infinite beings who make agreements to incarnate together in multiple lifetimes to assist one another in learning life lessons) to plan the next incarnation on Earth—a time between incarnations. During the pre-birth session a soul begins to plan the lesson it wishes to learn while in human form. In accordance with those lessons, the soul plans events to occur during the lifetime in order to learn those particular lessons.

The concept of the pre-birth planning is the basis for some of the healing lessons I have been able to experience. Upon my first reading, I found it very fascinating, and yet I was not so sure how to apply the concept to my life experiences. I had thoughts around the question, "What if this is true?"

What if I have indeed planned this lifetime, these lessons, and these experiences? What are the implications for what I have manifested thus far, in this lifetime?

My childhood experiences have caused a great deal of pain for me in my adult life so I started to answer these questions from there. I began by exploring my relationship with my father. At the time I believed I was in a good place with this relationship and was convinced I had healed much of the pain related to my parental issues. Applying the concept of "soul planning" helped me delve deeper into the relationship.

As an illegitimate child, I grew up with a great deal of pain around my absent father. My mother gave birth to three children with my father, of which I am the middle child. My father had two other children with his wife. In our younger years they lived a few blocks from us. He did manage to spend some nights in our household but my memories of those occasions are blurred.

I was very confused about the family dynamics of my early childhood days. With that confusion came a great deal of pain and anger toward my father, since he certainly did not honor any of his obligations to care for us three children. It was easy for me to see my half-siblings having their needs cared for; they had a nice home and clothing and attended better schools.

Witnessing the way he cared for his other family made me feel as if we were not worthy of his love. He wouldn't pay any child support and never contributed to the things we needed. Until after my mother sued him for child support—in the process we had to take a blood test to prove he was our father. I was at least thirteen years old, and his denial of paternity was just another blow.

Let me go back just a bit to the time before I was even aware of my father's identity. There was another father figure in my life—my maternal grandfather. The relationship, or lack thereof, with my biological father became evident later in my childhood.

My earliest childhood memories revolve around my relationship with my grandfather. In fact, I spent most of my early childhood with him. I have memories of him changing my diapers, feeding me my bottle, and dressing me. My mom tells me stories about my grandfather showing up early in the mornings to pick me up, and how she had to practically steal me away from him in the evenings. I even recall going with him to work building chain link and block fences. I would sit in his pickup truck and watch.

My grandfather spoiled me rotten. He gave me everything a little girl could need or want. I realized looking back how incredibly special the relationship was with my granddaddy. I was one of maybe forty (at the time) grandchildren; my grandparents had thirteen children of their own. The attention he gave to me was unprecedented, and to this day I have no idea how that came to be. What I do know is how much my life changed when he died.

I was seven years old when he passed away. He was sick for a few years before that with diabetes and high blood pressure. I remember the funeral like it was yesterday. There was a huge gathering, and I was sitting near the front of the church. It was an open-casket service, and from my seat I could see just a bit of his face if I lifted myself in my seat. When it was time for everyone to stand and walk past the casket for a final viewing and to say good-bye, I could not bring myself to go forward. I remember just sitting there in my seat as everyone paid their respects.

No one had explained to me what exactly was going on. I understood that he had gone to heaven, but there was no discussion or clarity around that for me. I don't recall feeling afraid, and I'm not sure that I even cried. What I know for sure is my life was never the same after his death.

It was after the death of my grandfather that I realized the huge disconnect from my family, except for my grandmother. She took more of an interest in me, and I believe it was because I reminded her of him. But no one cared for me the way my grandpa did; no one even came close.

Not long after my grandpa died my mother had a nervous breakdown. She was diagnosed with schizophrenia in her late twenties. Prior to her illness, my memories of her revolved around her relationship with my father and her partying all the time. She would get dressed up in her makeup and wigs; she would tell us kids she was going to the store but wouldn't come home until the next morning, with no groceries.

After her diagnosis, she stopped going out and stayed home with us instead. She didn't get dressed up as before, but would spend a good deal of time sleeping. She was depressed most of the time and was in and out of the hospital over the years. We moved in and out of my grandmother's home because my mother wasn't able to work or take care of us consistently without help.

It was a very difficult and confusing time for us kids. When she was having a manic episode she would do really strange things. She didn't sleep well at night and would sometimes roam the streets in the middle of the night. My grandmother tried to lock down the house but Mom would manage to escape somehow. There were many nights when my grandmother woke up my sister and me because my mother had left the house to roam the streets. She had us follow Mom to keep her safe and to get her to return home.

I was seven and my sister was nine years old. It was three or four in the morning, and we were following behind our mother as she paced up and down the streets of our neighborhood. She would knock on the neighbors' doors and talk nonsense to anyone who actually answered. It was embarrassing and frightening and happened more often than I care to talk about.

One night, my mom woke us kids and hade us kneel down on the floor with her. She prayed for God to take care of her kids. "God, please take care of my children because I am not able to." It was my first memory of accepting God into my life as a caretaker. She cried and prayed over us before allowing us to go back to bed.

My mind is unclear as to the exact timeline of events that occurred between the ages of –seven and fourteen. Each year seemed to blend into the next. We had to grow up quickly and had to take on adult responsibilities. Depending on the condition of my mother's health, we moved a lot but never far from my grandmother. We usually lived within a few houses or blocks from her. No matter where we lived, we were never in the house with just the four of us: my mom, sister, my brother, and me.

We lived in my grandmother's home for much of my childhood, which came with uncles, cousins, and countless other relatives in and out of the household. It never felt safe and

I learned to sleep with one foot on the floor. There were many male cousins around the house and I was molested, by several relatives, during some of those years.

It was accepted as part of my living condition. It was not done openly in front of the adults but we had teenage boys in and out of our house that touched and played games that were not appropriate. This happened often and with different relatives, and I still wonder to myself, where were the adults? Why wasn't anyone ever around to stop this from happening? I didn't know until years later that it wasn't just happening to me; my sister had been going through the same things.

I get that my mother was sick and unable to protect us but that doesn't take away the pain or the resentment. My level of self-worth deteriorated during those years. I felt unloved and uncared for. After the death of my grandfather I felt very alone in the world. My life was not the same after that and I often wondered to myself, what my life would have been like if he had not passed away. He was the only person who really showed me love and made me feel safe.

I lived this way for many years, accepting my living conditions as they were. I had no idea how to dream bigger dreams or how to create more in my life. I don't recall any incidents of molestation after the age of ten, and I'm not sure why or how it was stopped, but I'm grateful that it did. There were other challenges at that time in my life, however, that were just as undeniable.

My neighborhood was well known for drug abuse; everything from selling to using was part of my daily life. Many of my relatives were "caught up" and we spent many a weekend visiting jailhouses. It was like a field trip with promises of McDonald's for lunch if I agreed to ride along to visits to the prisons, which were always several hours from home.

The neighborhood talk was about who went to jail last night or who would be getting out soon. It didn't really matter because whoever went in or came out, would likely repeat the cycle over and over again. But this was all "normal" and part of daily life.

I spent a lot of time indoors. I would watch a lot from the windows because I didn't want to participate. My mom was still in and out of hospitals so most of my time was spent paying bills and taking care of household chores along with my sister. We cooked, cleaned, and did the laundry. We would cash Mom's disability checks at the local market and purchase money orders to pay the bills.

My younger brother was spoiled and protected by my mom. She somehow managed to downplay her manic episodes in his presence but didn't hold back for my sister or me. He was never able to see how sick she really was; he would always say "she's okay."

My sister and I were very close and shared in the responsibilities. We talked a lot about what we knew we didn't want for ourselves when were grown up. We were good students and had a few good teachers to guide us along the way. We were in music programs from early elementary school and continued through high school. I believe that music saved my life.

By the time I reached fourteen a few major events occurred. My sister moved out of the house and went to live with my uncle. She always had a close relationship with him; he was like a father to her. My mom was in and out of the hospital so we had to move back to my grandmother's house. We had a house full of people, and I would have to sleep with my grandmother.

There was one night in particular, my mom was in the hospital and I'm not sure where my grandmother was but my uncle was home with me and a few cousins where there. I don't recall what set me off but I got very upset and felt overwhelmed with my life circumstances. It was dark outside, and I remember storming past my uncle who had forbid us from leaving the house that night. I started to run down the street in search of my father.

I don't know what possessed me to do that or what it was I expected from him, but I was determined to find him. There was a house where the adults would hang out, so I was pretty sure I would find him there. I didn't know what I would say to him but I just felt like I wanted to be with him. Maybe I wanted him to hug me and say everything would be okay. It was an odd request because he had never done that for me before.

I ran up to the house, where many people were drinking, smoking, and dancing just as I had suspected. I saw him as soon as I reached the top step and immediately ran up to him. As soon as he saw me, he turned to me and said, "What do you want, I don't have any money." I didn't know what to say because I didn't go to him for money. He then said something along the lines of, "you need to go home."

I was in total shock because his response was hurtful and I had no idea why I had expected anything different. I didn't say anything to him or anyone else. I turned around and started walking back toward my grandmother's house. That night, I realized that I was on my own. My mom was unable to care for me, my sister had moved out, my brother, two years younger than me, was addicted to drugs, and my father couldn't hug me and tell me everything would be okay. I was on my own, and no one was going to rescue me. That was the moment I decided I was alone in the world and I was going to have to fend for myself.

There was a series of other events in my life that gave me evidence of how alone I really was. My sister went to college but returned home within two years. She had a nervous breakdown and was diagnosed with bipolar disorder. She was not the same person and we no longer connected like we had. She was no longer the big sister I looked up to. She had changed and was not able to be the strong one. My brother stayed in the drug scene and found trouble in the legal system. He is serving a life sentence in prison.

At the age of seventeen and on the morning of my high school graduation, I received my college acceptance letter to attend San Diego State University. I would finally have the opportunity to leave this lifestyle and discover something just for me. I started my first day of college on my eighteenth birthday. I did fairly well; I found a job in retail and eventually worked my way into a great paying management position.

For many years I did everything in my power to support my family financially, emotionally, and physically. I put everyone's need before my own, but I didn't feel worthy enough to want more for myself. I survived in this mode for many years before I learned to dream a bigger dream. I had to learn that life was more than surviving.

These are the challenges I have been working through as I mature. Through therapy and countless prayers around forgiveness I had managed to get by. I found a "good place" in my relationships and especially with my father. There was a time that I believed I was healed from the pain of our relationship. I attributed the lack of closeness to the fact that I didn't know him well and believed that was the cause of disconnect between us.

Deep inside I knew that wasn't the naked truth but it was good enough at the time. I could think of him and not be angry but there was still a deep-rooted longing for his love and protection. The recognition of residual pain was always present when someone mentioned him or when I ran into him at a family function, again providing evidence of some deeper issue. In fact, similar feelings of hurt and abandonment showed up in my relationships.

After reading *Your Soul's Plan,* I challenged myself to explore my relationship with my father. I set myself up by asking *If it is true, that I planned the relationship I have with my father, then what was the lesson I intended to learn?* The rules I applied to this exploration were that I would be completely honest with myself and that I would only view the experiences from my own perspective.

I utilized four guiding principles to act as rules for revealing the deepest truth available to me at the time. I stress, "at the time" because I know now that what is the deepest truth I can understand today may not be the deepest tomorrow, next week, or next year. Our truths become clearer as we grow in our wisdom. So these are the guiding principles in my process:

TRUTH: To identify the root cause of self-limiting thoughts and beliefs.

INTEGRITY: To identify and strengthen moral character.

COURAGE: To strengthen the mind, empowering a person to face difficulties

LOVE: To live without fear and honor our connection to ourselves and others

With these four principles I reached a turning point in how I viewed my relationship with my father. What if my father's main role in my life was to play the part of the male so I could be born? What if his role was to play a small part at certain times in my life for the purpose of triggering reactions in me, which then caused me to make certain decisions about my life?

Using the guiding principles of truth, integrity, courage, and love, I looked inside myself and started to ask a series of questions. I imagined what my life would have been like if he had played a different role. What is the truth about his role in my life? If he had been there for me as a father, what different decisions would I have made? What would my life look like had we had both played different roles?

The truth is that I wouldn't be who am I today without those moments, triggers, or turning points. His absence as a father allowed me to experience my childhood from a different perspective. I had to make decisions at an early age about who I wanted to be as I grew up. Early on I developed the virtue of integrity—a set morale principle to hold myself accountable without judging others.

The experiences caused me to know what I didn't want for my life, allowing me to dream about what I did want. I developed the courage to learn the lessons of love, relationships, and self-worth. I developed my mind and spirit to face pain and difficulties—to be brave.

Taking on the challenges of viewing my relationship with my father from this perspective was a very profound experience to say the least. I went from having pain in my heart to having the joyful feeling of gratitude. I learned to love him unconditionally and with extreme compassion.

I'm so grateful that he agreed to play this role knowing the pain he would cause me during this lifetime. My hope is that his soul is also learning the lessons he intended by playing the role. With truth, integrity, courage and love, I thank him.

From this point forward, I have applied these guiding principles to each area of my life and have experienced major shifts in all of them. When I experience moments of pain, confusion, or hurt, I no longer play the role of the victim. Instead I take the stance of the warrior by asking, what does my soul want to learn from this experience? I allow the feeling to happen. Not for the sake of pain but for the healing effects of the experience itself.

All of this leads me to what I call, the TICL Effect. It is the process through which I reconcile my deepest truths having to do with my relationships. I discovered that it works in every area of my life. The TICL Effect is a set of guiding principles that, when accessed properly, can yield amazing, life-transforming results. The TICL Effect has impacted my thinking mind, body, and relationships, especially with myself. The TICL Effect changed how I choose to be in the world.

In the following chapters I will share stories around my personal transformation and the virtues of TICL, which brought clarity and healing in to my life. There were several turning points along my path, and I will do my best to share in a way that will allow your own truths and healing to come forth. At the beginning of each chapter I will share a quote with you that was given to me through spiritual connections that have guided me along my journey.

CHAPTER 1: THE TICL EFFECT

"You are Limitless"

FOR THE PAST SEVERAL YEARS I have journeyed from "having" everything I wanted to not having much of anything. From having a beautiful home, money, and great investments etc., to having a failing business, losing my home, and having to ask friends for a place to live.

My intention is to share my authentic self and what I have experienced in the hopes of inspiring you to make positive changes in your life. This is simply my journey and the incredible twists and turns along my path. Most importantly, I want to share who I met along the way. First and foremost, I was introduced to my higher-self—the inner person I've always been, but had no clue how to access.

Along this path and through great teachers I was introduced to a fabulous family of divine helpers. I was made aware of angels, spirit guides, ascended masters, and guardian angels. It is important for me to share this information because my journey has been blessed by their presence.

In addition, much of what I will discuss is divinely channeled and directed through my connection to these divine helpers. You are certainly not required to share my beliefs, I only hope you enjoy and appreciate what I am called to share.

At the age of ninety-four, my grandmother passed away. As I explained in the beginning of my story, she played a very significant role in my life growing up. A few years before she passed she had become ill and was no longer her vibrant self. The last time I spoke with her while she was alive, she only recognized me for a few moments before she "disappeared." I stopped visiting her after that experience.

It was difficult for me to see her in that condition, and I was intuitively aware she was no longer present in her body. In that brief moment when she did remember who I was, there was a connection between the two of us. I was assured we would always be connected.

A few months before her passing she began to visit me during my morning meditations. The first time I became aware of her presence was through the sound of her voice and the feeling that she was next to me. I could feel her presence so strongly that I started to cry from pure joy.

I told her how sorry I was that I had not been to visit her and how badly I felt for not wanting to see her in her illness. She consoled me and explained that she was okay and although her body appeared to deteriorate, she was not suffering. Her soul had left her earthly body; what was there was only the body. Over the next few months she would periodically visit me and we shared beautiful moments together. From there I met my great-grandmother, whom I had never before met. She passed away before I was born.

The energy or spirit of my great-grandmother is very powerful. When she wants to make herself known all goes still around the moment. She introduced herself to me during the few months before my grandmother passed. She explained that she was waiting for my grandmother to completely pass over. When that happened, they would be together and would be helping me to align with and live my life's purpose.

About two weeks before my earthly grandmother passed away, she visited with me and told me it was close to time for her to exit. She asked me to call my aunt who had been her caregiver throughout her illness. She was concerned that my aunt would have a difficult time with her passing and also that my aunt was feeling some guilt about her illness. As I was ending this session with my granny I heard the date September 11th. We were in the beginning of September 2011 and the 11th is significant to us all so I dismissed it as insignificant to her visit.

On Friday, September 9, 2011 I flew out to New Mexico to spend the weekend with friends in Santa Fe. We had a great visit but in the back of my mind I couldn't shake the voice that announced to me the date "September 11th." On the morning of September 11, 2011, I was due to fly home and being on a plane on that particular date, especially after hearing that particular message was a bit disconcerting. I didn't feel in danger, however, so I proceeded as planned.

When I landed in San Diego, I turned on my cell phone and within seconds my messages started to come in. The first was a missed called, the second was a voice message, and the third was a text message. The messages were from my aunt, and they said, "Granny passed away today." In that moment, I experienced the greatest evidence of all of what was happening around me. My grandmother had given me the date of her passing two weeks earlier. You cannot prepare enough for the passing of a loved one, and I could not have prepared for what occurred next.

After the funeral services when family members had gone back to their usual routines, myself included, I had another visit from my grandmothers. This time they were together along with a third person, whose identity has not been clearly revealed to me, just that she is the youngest of the three. From that point until now, my great-grandmother does the speaking during these visits.

She explained to me that my grandmother was with her and they were there, as she had promised, to work with me as my guides. They also shared information with me about my true lineage and my soul group. She said that my earthly family was not my soul family and this is why I never fit in. I come from a tribe of ancient healers called the Essene and I, with their help, would bring some of the ancient teachings into modern times.

At the time this information was given to me I had no idea who the Essene were. Immediately afterward, I began a journey to find out. What I learned was amazing. I will share briefly that:

1. The Essenes are believed to have authored the Dead Sea Scrolls;

2. The Essenes were a tribe of powerful healers who worked with the angels to perform miraculous healings using the power of words; and
3. Joseph, Mary, John the Baptist and Jesus were Essenes.

It is not my purpose to persuade you one way or the other about the accuracy of the information found online or in books. I am sharing with you what is relevant to what I am experiencing along my journey. Should you seek information on you own you will discover the controversy surrounding the Essene.

From this point forward, when I refer to my grandmothers, I am referencing a collective consciousness of divine helpers (spirit guides, angels, and ascended masters).

I absorbed all of what my grandmother shared and all of what I learned as I researched the information. My grandmothers have continually shared with me divine insights about life and how to navigate through it. It has been said in many ways that we are souls having a human experience, and this has been the foundation for the teachings I have received. My grandmothers have given me, as a form of structure, the following topics loosely based on a portion of the Essene Sevenfold Peace:

- Peace with the Body
- Peace with the Mind
- Peace with Relationships
- Peace with Humanity

As I mentioned, my grandmothers offered these as a structure, therefore I will not go into detail about the teachings of the Sevenfold Peace. I will offer this as a modern-day template for how we are operating in current times. At the beginning of each chapter I will share a message from my grandmothers as it relates to each topic. I encourage you to keep an open mind as these revelations may lead you down a path different than what I experienced.

Before we go into each of these areas it is critical to share more background information that will tie all of this together as it relates to the TICL Effect. As I was led to revisit the topic of pre-birth planning what I learned was that the lessons we chose to experience for our Soul's growth are called divine virtues or spiritual qualities. Here is a short list, of many, lessons a soul may chose to learn:

Acceptance	Independence
Beauty	Humility
Discipline	Truth
Courage	Spirituality
Ethics	Love
Compassion	Patience
Harmony	Integrity

There are an unlimited number of qualities a soul may wish to experience for its own growth. Through the virtues of truth, integrity, courage, and love, I have been able to create a system that promotes growth in all areas of life. We are souls having a human experience for the purpose of awakening to our true authentic selves. The TICL process helps us to remember who we truly are through self-discovery—a transformation from within.

Release all limiting thoughts, feelings and beliefs because in Truth, "You are limitless."

For those who wish to hear.

CHAPTER 2: BODY

"What you are looking for, you will find in Church."

WHEN I HEARD THESE WORDS I went on a search for the true meaning of what my grandmothers intended for me to learn. There are similar sayings in the teachings of Jesus. From reading the Bible and other books on Jesus' teachings I immediately questioned the word "church." Was this a physical church or was this a metaphorical church. In order to fully understand I had to explore the possibilities.

The first was to visit a few "physical churches" to see if my grandmothers were directing me to get involved with a church. I grew up going to church with my family and my earthly grandmother was very involved in her church while she was here. So, I explored a few options by scheduling to attend services at three different churches. Each of the selected churches had very different philosophies, styles, and audiences. I performed my due diligence; I went to service, participated at my highest possible level, and honestly enjoyed each service for various reasons. However, there was no resonance with the message I had been given.

The Bible was my next source of information, so I searched for the passages that spoke about church. I came across a reference that says something along the lines of Jesus being the Church. The body of Christ being the church made sense after a bit more research. It was a concept believed by many and resonated closer to the message I heard, but it wasn't totally there. In fact, I felt more certain that the message had a deeper meaning.

At this point in the process I started to realize the only way to get a deeper meaning was to go within. To ask my grandmothers for clarity about why the message was given, and what I was to learn from it. What came from this was a gradual learning that occurred over many months, via many books, classes, conversations with spiritual teachers, and other modes of discovery. The most reflective insights came to me while I was becoming certified as a Reiki II Practitioner.

During class I was learning how to move energy with my hands for the purpose of healing. The healings were taking place physically and emotionally within my own body. I started to give myself treatments as a way to balance my chakras and stimulate the flow of energy through my body. This was the first time I had done any work on my body through this spiritual and energetic type of healing. My grandmothers began pointing out particular blocks in my body. Some were physical blocks and some were emotional, especially around my heart and stomach.

When this was shown to me over and over again I finally had my moment of clarity. The areas around my heart and my stomach were also the areas where I have the tendency to carry extra weight on my body. It was always fascinating to me that my weight fluctuated but always seemed to rest in these areas. No matter how much I ate (or not), exercised and so on, I always kept on the extra pounds in this area.

At this point I knew there was a connection among the message, the energy healing, and the weight. From this, I determined that the "church" to which my grandmothers were referring was my own body. For me, this revelation was huge because it led me to take a closer look at the dynamics of my own body. The energy work was calling to my attention the toxins I was carrying in my body. As I did the work, the toxins began to be released from my body in amazing and varying ways.

While experiencing these releases, my grandmothers continued with the lesson and explained the importance of the physical body. How we must treat our bodies as temples. Our bodies are vehicles for connection to the divine that is always present. When our physical bodies are filled with toxins—physical, mental, and spiritual toxins—we are not able to receive a clear connection to Source. We must accept our bodies as they are and treat them with respect. We get one body in this lifetime, and how we chose to operate within our body will determine the level of growth and evolution we experience.

When I learned the truth about my body and its purpose, I was given the option to choose how I wanted to respond. My investment at this stage was deep, so I chose to continue with the learning—I chose to act with integrity. I had to ask myself the question, did I have the courage to make the changes I knew I would be asked to make? Did I love myself enough to make them?

Physical changes within my body occurred next. I learned that when we are stressed, burdened, or have low self-esteem, one of the ways our bodies react is to build excess weight especially around the heart (heart chakra/love) and stomach (solar plexus/power center). The body does this on a physical level but the source is mental, emotional, and spiritual. As I began to embrace the truth that my body is a temple, and that I am a soul having a human experience, my body changed. The weight started to come off before I implemented any changes in my diet or exercise program.

I got honest with myself about my internal issues around self-worth and wondering whether I was worthy of receiving information from the divine. But when I embraced the possibilities that were presented, that I am truly divine, I was shown the evidence. The more I honored my truth, acted with integrity and courage, and started to love and honor myself, the more weight came off. Then my cravings around food changed; my body wanted more fruits and vegetables. Junk food, snacks, and dairy products were not as desirable. I occasionally enjoy my treats, but I no longer crave them as a source of emotional comfort.

This is an ongoing process for me, but the great starting point was to begin accepting my body just as it is. I started to love the extra weight, and I thanked it for the protection it provided when I needed it. Through my energy work, I am releasing it as it is no longer needed. I talk to my body, and I'm sculpting it into the desirable temple I want.

Ultimately, my connection to my grandmothers became clearer and more frequent. My healing with Reiki was amplified, and other healing gifts emerged. I encourage you to spend some time with your body. Breathe deeply and listen to the messages your body is giving you. If you are healthy, listen to the ease with which you breathe, feel the strength of every muscle, and see the glow of your skin. If you are not healthy, listen deeply for difficulties in breathing, fatigue, skin outbreaks, or other outward symbols of imbalance. Your body is a temple and will speak to you if you let it.

"What you are looking for, you will find in Church."

For those who wish to hear.

CHAPTER 3: MIND

"Silence is a high vibration(al) way of thinking."

MY GIFTS ARE NO GREATER than anyone else's. I have learned to hear messages from my grandmothers through a process to which I have committed myself. The only difference between someone who can hear these types of messages and someone who cannot hear them is the level of their commitment to being silent.

These messages have been coming to me for many years, and some I received before I had any idea what to do with them. The lessons I'm sharing with you have been organized for the purpose of sharing, but the truth is these messages that have revealed themselves at different turning points along my journey. There are times when a message comes and, for a while, there are no clear revelations. Each message has taken me on a journey to uncover divine gifts and promote self-healing.

I started to keep a dream journal when I realized my dream time had become more vivid. There were many years when I had no recollection of dreaming at all. I have come to understand that once you commit to learning, the divine guides will find ways to communicate with you. My guidance started to come in the form of dreams. The messages from my grandmothers have one thing in common: I received each at the moment just before becoming fully awake—a time when the mind is silent.

I remember one morning in particular when I was meditating but my mind was going on and on. At one point a voice said, "Stop talking." I recognized the voice of my earthly grandmother, and I immediately stopped the chatter in my head. I just sat there like a child in trouble, but what followed immediately was a beautiful silence. A peace that was loving, gentle, and kind. I sat in that space for a few moments, and then it was gone. Needless to say, I wanted it back.

My meditation at that time was informal and somewhat effective but not anything like what I experienced in those moments with my grandmother. That led me to seek more formal methods of meditation, and HeartMath was a form that suited me for a while. I was able to have those moments, but again, they weren't consistent, and I wanted to experience the silence that I shared with my grandmother.

The truth is that I was not a good listener. I spent most of my meditation time planning out my day. There were moments of actual meditation, but I had a good amount of chatter going on—and I was answering it. I truly wanted to embrace my grandmothers' message and to hear at the highest level of divine vibrations available. I was concerned because I had heard stories and seen movies about spirits taking over bodies and giving messages, but I gathered the courage with the trust that I would be divinely guided and protected.

I continued to seek and study various forms of meditation and was divinely guided to Transcendental Meditation. The amount of research and evidence of the positive effects of TM is available everywhere. The experience of TM is a very personal experience for each individual in practice therefore, I could not begin to share on any deep level what it is. I do know for me, the silence and peace I experienced in that moment with my grandmother is available to me, twice a day, when I meditate.

Since I began practicing TM, the clarity of truth for me, my speech, and my thought has shifted to create more positive results in my life. The illusions and meanings I gave to "things" no longer plague me. My filter for what is relevant and what is irrelevant in my life works for me and not against me. The study and process is cumulative, and the journey is incredible. I have learned that a true meditative practice requires integrity and commitment. To take on any such practice is a gift to the self and a beautiful expression of self love.

"Silence is a high vibration(al) way of thinking."

For those who wish to hear.

CHAPTER 4: RELATIONSHIPS

"Speak for those who cannot speak for themselves."

When I was initially given the message from my grandmothers to "speak for those who cannot speak for themselves," I wasn't really sure what it meant. So again I started out on the journey to understand the message that was so divinely given to me by my grandmothers. I initially thought I was being told that I need to advocate for those who were abused, disenfranchised, or even homeless. Or perhaps it was to work on behalf of women and children who have been abused in various ways. I had no experience as an advocate for others, especially as it relates to abuse or homelessness, but I was determined to understand the message.

A week or so after hearing the message I was attending service at church where the reverend led us in a meditation. The meditation was designed to help us identify the person who we identified as the "betrayer" in our life. He prefaced the meditation by explaining that the person in our life who we may see as someone who has betrayed us or caused us pain may actually be the person who likely volunteered, during the pre-birth planning session, to play this role for us. The purpose in playing the role was to trigger more pain in our lives in order for us to reveal and heal past hurts.

The reverend started to walk us through the meditation step-by-step. In the scenario in which we would play out the meditation I found myself sitting in a room with all white walls, a white table in the center surrounded by white chairs. I felt a deep relaxation as he continued the guided mediation.

I pictured in my mind every detail of the words he shared, and soon I was feeling quite peaceful and content in my environment. The next step in the meditation was to invite in the person we would identify as the betrayer. That person entered a door, approached the table, and sat across from me. At that moment something really amazing happened: two young girls entered from behind me and sat down on either side of me. To my left was a seven year old version of me and to my right was a fourteen year old girl, another version of me.

The person across from me sat down, and within moments I recognized this person to be my mother. At this point in the meditation I was a bit confused because my experience was already proving to be different than what I had expected. I was surprised to find my mother as my betrayer and was extremely surprised to see versions of myself joining in the meditation.

Recognizing these young ladies as versions of myself caused an emotional uprising within my heart. An emotion I can't say I had felt before, especially looking across the table and recognizing my mother as someone that I internally viewed as my betrayer. I have challenges with my mother and our relationship, but I never would have identified her consciously as the one who betrayed me. However when the two young versions of me sat down, the need for deep healing became much clearer.

The young girls were in pain, and when I recognized the level of hurt inside of me, I knew this was a moment where healing was being called forth. Those girls were asking for healing that I didn't understand was necessary until that moment. For the remainder of the meditation I found myself holding their hands and comforting these young versions of myself.

I assured them that they were safe and the things that happened then were not their fault. I apologized for not being strong enough to protect them the way they needed to be protected. We hugged and embraced, and the three of us blended into one whole being. We, my little girls and me, then looked across the table, and we forgave our mom for not being the mother we needed while growing up. It was an amazing breakthrough in my journey to healing.

I look back at the words my grandmother had given me, "speak for those who cannot speak for themselves," and by the end of that meditation I committed to always speak for those little girls who lived inside of me. They didn't know how to speak up for themselves, and they didn't know that the life they were living was not the ideal life. Until that day I didn't know that I carried those feelings into my adult life.

"Speak for those who cannot speak for themselves" was a call for me to look inside myself and speak for the little girls who had no voice. I was called to remember the hurt and pain that dwelled within my heart. I understood the truth of these little girls living in my body and mind, and they were showing up in my relationships. I was always seeking love outside of myself when the love I needed has always been internal.

I cried and cried during this meditation. I had not understood up to this point how much I truly hurt. I'd been working diligently to heal myself, but until then, I didn't fully grasp how much of my past, especially my childhood, was buried in the depths of my being. I remembered an excerpt of a poem I had read by Iyanla Vanzant:

> Yesterday, I cried, for all the days that I was too busy, or too tired, or too mad to cry. I cried for all the days, and all the ways, and all the times I had dishonored, disrespected, and disconnected my *self* from myself, only to have it reflected back to me in the ways others did to me the same things I had already done to myself.
>
> I cried for all the things I had given, only to have them stolen; for all the things I had asked for that had yet to show up; for all the things I had accomplished, only to give them away, to people in circumstances, which left me feeling empty, and battered and plain old used.
>
> I cried because there really does come a time when the only thing left for you to do is cry.
>
> Yesterday, I cried. I cried because little boys get left by their daddies; and little girls get forgotten by their mommies; and daddies don't know what to do, so they leave; and mommies get left, so they get mad.

I cried because I had a little boy, and because I was a little girl, and because I was a mommy who didn't know what to do, and because I wanted my daddy to be there so badly until I ached.

Yesterday, I cried.

I cried because I hurt. I cried because I was hurt. I cried because hurt has no place to go except deeper into the pain that caused it in the first place, and when it gets there, the hurt wakes you up.

(Vanzant 2000, 17-18)

I went home after service, and I continued to cry until I hurt all over. This was a new truth that had been revealed, and I was led to seek a deeper level of learning about myself. The integrity of who I believed I was had been shattered. It took a great deal of courage to face the possibilities that because of the old hurts, I didn't truly love myself. I put everyone's need before my own, and the evidence was placed in front of me. I had to learn to love myself enough, to speak on behalf of the young girls who had no voice or explanation for the wrongs committed against them.

Learning about my relationship with my self has been an ongoing process. I still find myself in situations where I'm giving so freely of myself that I forget to receive. The difference now is I recognize when I am playing small, and I work toward healing myself in those situations. I now value myself above all others and remain committed to hearing the voice of my inner child.

I have learned to "speak for those who cannot speak for themselves," and I wish the same for you.

For those who wish to hear.

CHAPTER 5: HUMANITY

"Banish all Thoughts of Separateness"

AT THIS STAGE I AM fully on board and committed to my spiritual journey. I was practicing my listening techniques and gaining insight in every area of my life. I eagerly anticipated any new information knowing my life would be enhanced by whatever was given. When my grandmothers gave me this message however, I felt inadequate in my attempt to grasp the concept. In order to "banish all thoughts of separateness" I had to have the thought that I was separate.

This message came to me while I was having some difficulties at my job. Although I loved what I was doing, I wasn't growing or learning anything new. It is my nature to strive for perfection, and in this case I felt hampered and held back. I wasn't thriving on a daily basis, at least not through my work. The internal chatter told me that it was my bosses' fault for not giving me enough authority and that it was my bosses' fault for not acting on my suggestions. The blame game was in full swing.

I applied my wisdom immediately knowing from experience that anytime my grandmothers gave me a message it was directly related to areas in which I needed to grow. In this case I was having serious issues in my work and not just the work itself, but in particular with my relationships with my bosses. So I sat down with myself and meditated on what it would look like if indeed there were a connection between the message "banish all of the separateness" and my challenge at work.

The truth of the matter surfaced fairly quickly. The fact that I could blame my bosses for my unhappiness at work was evidence that I saw myself as being separate from them. Over the years I had read quite a few books that spoke about oneness and about how we, as individuals, are related to one another through humanity. In fact I remembered when reading about our soul planning, that we are elevating our own growth while impacting that of our soul group, as well as, all of humanity.

Tying this information together was absolutely eye-opening for me. I immediately realized that the blame game was not serving me or my work situation. There is no integrity in the blame game and I needed to own that for myself and take responsibility for making changes that would better serve me. This was a very difficult process for me because I had played the blame game for so long I had no idea how to do anything differently.

The first commitment I made to myself was to pay attention to the feelings generated in those moments where the chatter in my mind started to play the blame game. I realized I was judging people in ways that were clearly caused by the belief that I was separate from them. Through further studies I learned that the judgments that I was placing on them were really reflections of myself. That moment of realization was jaw dropping for me. I had already done so much internal work to heal issues related to self-worth. Now I'm gaining an understanding that there are deeper levels related to self-worth in terms of how we see other people, and how that becomes a challenge for our self-perception.

I realized I wasn't mad or angry with my bosses. I was angry with myself because I had settled into a position that I knew was not serving my highest good. From there I was able to shift from the blaming others to taking full responsibility for my own happiness. In doing so my focus shifted to being present when I was working in my job in order to maintain complete integrity. Outside of my job I found new ways of challenging myself to grow and evolve on a personal level as well as ways to get into alignment with my life's purpose.

There was such an incredible amount of joy in putting these thoughts and feelings into action. When I started to see myself as part of the whole and not separate from others, judgments began to diminish. Not just the judgment of others but more profoundly the judgments I had of myself. For me this is still a work in progress. And what I now know is that I have gathered the courage necessary to align myself with my life purpose.

The Essene teach that each of us travels a very unique spiritual path in serving all of human evolution, and it is only when we pursue our own unique contributions that joy and peace will rein in our societies. So we each have a responsibility to ourselves and to our fellow human beings to do our best by aligning with our life purpose. To stop playing the blame game and take responsibility to make changes that lead to balance, peace, and harmony. It takes courage to step outside of our comfort zone of blaming others for our circumstances. However, when we love ourselves enough we will take whatever actions necessary to learn how to take full responsibility and ownership of our happiness.

One of the most powerful steps we can take to align with our life's purpose is to recognize our unique gifts. Embrace the unique gifts we were born with and have committed to utilizing for our own growth and for the growth of others. I found my gift in words.

When people engage me in conversation they tend to share with me more information than I would have solicited from them during a first meeting. There was a time when I walked away from those interactions because I felt they were violations of my personal space. Through my studies I have identified my gift of discernment which has led to emotional healings. I have the unique ability to listen and hear things that others do not hear—the words behind the words.

When I am engaged in conversation with a person there is a process taking place where my mind is separating the facts from the emotion or judgment. I am able to "hear" when a person is in pain, even when the hurt appears irrelevant to the topic being shared. I hear the words behind the words and notice the underlying emotion being spoken. I then respond in a way that leads to revealing emotional truths which lead to healing.

Utilizing my gift of discernment allows me to separate the emotion from the facts and take a different course of action. I ask relevant questions to break down the situation until we get to the emotional issue that is really the root of the problem. Learning to embrace my gift has made me open and receptive to healing myself and others. I no longer see others sharing their problems as a burden. I see an opportunity to contribute to my own healing and the healing of others.

Embracing my gifts has allowed me to focus my energy in a positive way. As a healer and spiritual coach I take great pleasure in utilizing my gifts to create harmony and balance. With the help of my grandmothers I have been able to recognize and accept my spiritual gifts and to help others reveal their own.

It is my greatest joy to be in relationship with individuals working to identify their gifts and to watch them grow and evolve to the point where they begin to share their learning with others. All of this information is available to us when we embrace our gifts and align ourselves with our true life purpose. In doing our own work we create peace and harmony for ourselves and humanity as a whole.

From that point of view an even deeper truth revealed itself; we are not separate from Source or from God. The truth is no matter what our life experience we are perfect and whole just as we are. We are here to learn, develop, and evolve our spirit which is also the spirit of God internal. We are not our experience but are spiritual beings having this human experience. When you look at it from this perspective the illusions that we call our life, begin to disappear.

When we consider and accept our humanity as not separate from our divinity, we begin to live life in a whole new light. The challenges and the difficulties become opportunities to grow. Not that they become easier but that they become life lessons, and we begin to understand them and become less reactive to them. We stop struggling with them and learn to direct ourselves in a new way. We remember who we are and become the incredible co-creators that we truly are. Life no longer "happens" to us. We practice truth, integrity, courage, and love and allow the spirit of all that is to flow through us.

Imagine this: everything we could ever want and need is already available to us. When we pray to God to bring us this or that, He tells us that it's already there. All you have to do is align yourself with what it is you want, and it will appear before you. We are not separate from our Source, we are our Source. We are everything we want to be, and we have everything we want to have. We are here to remember who we are. Go inside yourself and listen to the whispering voice that is always present and alert within ourselves—our divine connection.

It is there when we "Banish all Thoughts of Separateness."

For those who wish to hear.

CONCLUSION

Your Original Face

Jesus said, "Take no thought from the morning until the evening and from the evening until the morning, for what you shall put on."

His disciples said, "When wilt thou be revealed to us and when will we see thee?"

Jesus said, "When you take off your clothing without being ashamed, and take your clothes and put them under your feet as the little children and tread on them—then shall you behold the son of the living one, and you shall not fear." (Osho 2009, 65)

I shared this excerpt in the beginning of the book, and I'm sharing it again now to underscore why this project is so important to me. There have been countless interpretations of what the parables of Jesus really mean. Osho brings a clear understanding to the powerful words Jesus spoke. Osho says:

> Man lives not as he is but as he would to be: not with the original face, but with a painted, false face. That is the whole problem. When you are born you have a face of your own – nobody has disturbed it, nobody has changed it – but

sooner or later the society starts working on your face. It starts hiding the original, the natural, the one you were born with, and then many faces are given to you to for different occasions because one face won't do.

Situations change so you need many false faces, masks. From the morning till the evening, from the evening till the morning, thousands of faces are used. When you see a man approaching who is powerful, you change your mask; when you see a man who is a beggar approaching you, you are different. The whole time, moment to moment, there is a constant change in the face.(Osho 2009, 65)

There was an incredible truth revealed to me in these passages. I went to bed the night I read them with the words on my mind. I had a dream so profound that I want to share it with you now.

I was on a yacht in the San Diego Harbor. (I could see the Coronado Bridge.) The skyline was absolutely brilliant, the lights of downtown glowing, and the stars took my breath away. On top of all that, there were fireworks all over the sky. I was on this yacht playing the role of the receptionist, signing in the guests as they boarded the boat.

The boat was already out in the harbor, so the guests were arriving via helicopter (landing on the water), speed boats, and rafts. As the guests boarded the yacht, I would greet them and sign them in. They were all showing up in costume—from Humpty Dumpty to various super heroes. They signed in names like Electra Star and Superman, among others.

It was not a costume party, so I had a feeling of confusion as to why they were showing up in character. After a while, I noticed myself, and I was the only person on the boat not in character. This added to my confusion as more guests arrived.

I woke up the next morning and scribbled down the dream in my journal and went about my normal routine. Throughout the day bits and pieces of the dream drifted in and out of my mind. I always came back to me and my lack of costume. That night, I went back to *The Mustard Seed* and read the passage again.

When we reach out and ask for knowledge and understanding, Spirit always says yes. The dream was Spirit providing me with a living example of what it means to wear the masks and to see the masks of others. In dream interpretation there were many clues to the many positive aspects of the dream (yacht, helicopter, and fireworks, etc.) that demonstrated I was on the right path in discarding my many masks. The fact that I was the only person without a mask was evidence that the direction I had been going was the right one.

For years I have been asking Spirit for guidance and running with every bit of guidance I receive. Being my true authentic self has been my path to evolving and this was another beautiful turning point along my path. Taking a lifetime of events and working through each of the masks is a struggle. We are in essence letting go of a part of who we thought we were— mom, dad, sister, boss, student, teacher, or friend.

What we are really seeking is to be our true, authentic selves. We really want "to be naked and not ashamed." We want to take off our many masks and restore our natural selves, just as little children, just as we were born. Remember who we are and know, deeply know, we are not our experiences. We are not all the "bad" things that "happened" to us.

We are perfect and whole as we have always been. We designed our experiences for our soul's growth. Every person, place, and circumstance was perfectly ordered and executed by us for us.

There are five responses I give to people when they feel they are in crisis:

- You have choices.
- Practice forgiveness.
- You are not a victim.
- Open your heart to receive love.
- This is an opportunity to grow.

These responses are not always welcoming, but they will immediately take you on the path to remembrance. We start to take off the masks one at a time and start down the path of remembering our grace. We recognize our divinity, our humanity, and our true authentic selves. When we take the five responses above and infuse them with truth, integrity, courage, and love, we begin an incredible journey toward healing ourselves.

"Be Naked and Not Ashamed"

When we learn to peel ourselves away from the drama, we get to simply be with ourselves. When we pretend to be someone other than who we are, we feel stressed and fake. We don't have to be one way at home and a different way at work.

We can be our true authentic selves wherever we are. For many people these ideas are frightening, but imagine first what it would feel like. Sit with yourself as you are when you feel the most like yourself. Take that person on a journey through your day, and do not switch the mask. How might your day be different? How much more joy do you see in your day?

Getting to this point takes a lot of work. You must be willing to face your fears over and over as deeper levels are revealed through your work. The TICL Effect is a transformational process for getting through this transformation.

"Pressing on Toward the Goal"

The apostle Paul says, "Not that I have already obtained all this, or have already been made perfect, but I press on to take hold of that for which Christ Jesus took hold of me. Brother, I do not consider myself yet to have taken hold of it. But one thing I do: Forgetting what is behind and straining toward what is ahead, I press on toward the goal to win the prize for which God has called me heavenward in Christ Jesus" –(Philippians 3:12-14).

I do not claim, as Paul says, to have made perfect for myself all that I have shared with you. I do claim that I am committed to living this lifetime gracefully and fully. I will continue to grow, develop, and evolve as I intended to do when I planned this incarnation. I am committed to moving forward toward my Heaven on Earth.

TICL (TRUTH.INTEGRITY.COURAGE.LOVE) INSTITUTE™

At TICL (Truth.Integrity.Courage.Love) Institute™, we lead you step by step through The TICL Effect™.

Truth: Identify the root cause of self-limiting thoughts and beliefs

Integrity: Identify and strengthen moral character

Courage: Strengthen the mind that enables a person to face difficulties

Love: Live without fear and honor our connection to ourselves and others

These are the divine virtues I have found useful in my personal process for gaining wisdom. I apply these four virtues to every area of my life and have had amazing results. I am divinely guided to share the details and the process with you in hopes that you will also gain inner wisdom.

When applied in a natural order, inner truths are revealed for the purpose of healing. When applied openly, as our true authentic selves, a deep and profound healing takes place within. You will need courage to enter into such a process, but the courage you gain is a different courage than what you started with. The love you acquire is a deeper love of self.

This is my invitation to you to join us at TICL (Truth. Integrity.Courage.Love) Institute. This transformational journey of self-discovery is conducted with a tremendous amount of unconditional love. No judgments and no masks.

For those who wish to hear.

REFERENCES

Osho. 2009. *The Mustard Seed: The Revolutionary Teachings of Jesus*. New York: OSHO Medial International.

Schwartz, Robert. 2009. *Your Soul's Plan: Discovering the Real Meaning of the Life You Planned Before You Were Born*. Berkeley, California: North Atlantic Books, Frog Books.

The Student Bible, New International Version. Grand Rapids, Michigan: Zondervan Corporation, 1996.

Vanzant, Iyanla. 2000. *Yesterday I Cried: Celebrating the Lessons of Living and Loving*. New York: Simon & Schuster.